THIS BOOK BELONGS ...

CONTACT INFORMATION

NAME:	
ADDRESS:	
PHONE:	

START / END DATES

_____ / _____ / _____   TO   _____ / _____ / _____

POOL MAINTENANCE LOG

POOL/CLIENT NAME		DATE	
LOCATION		POOL SIZE	
FLOW RATE REQUIRED		DISINFECTANT TYPE	

DAILY TEST	TIME (AM/PM)						
	WATER CLARITY						
	DISINFECTANT PPM						
	COMBINED CHLORINE <50% FREE						
	PH 7.2-8.0						
	FLOW GPM						

WEEKLY TEST	ALKALINITY REC RANGE 60-160 PPM						
	CYANURIC ACID IF USED - < 90						

CHEMICALS ADDED	QTY OF DISINFECTANT ADDED						
	OTHER CHEMICALS ADDED						

POOL MAINTENANCE LOG

POOL/CLIENT NAME		DATE	
LOCATION		POOL SIZE	
FLOW RATE REQUIRED		DISINFECTANT TYPE	

DAILY TEST	TIME (AM/PM)					
	WATER CLARITY					
	DISINFECTANT PPM					
	COMBINED CHLORINE <50% FREE					
	PH 7.2-8.0					
	FLOW GPM					

WEEKLY TEST	ALKALINITY REC RANGE 60-160 PPM					
	CYANURIC ACID IF USED - < 90					

CHEMICALS ADDED	QTY OF DISINFECTANT ADDED					
	OTHER CHEMICALS ADDED					

POOL MAINTENANCE LOG

MAINTENANCE		
BACKWASH	VACUUM AND/OR BRUSH	CONTAMINANT EPISODE
	☐VACUUM ☐BRUSH	
	☐VACUUM ☐BRUSH	
	☐VACUUM ☐BRUSH	
	☐VACUUM ☐BRUSH	
	☐VACUUM ☐BRUSH	
	☐VACUUM ☐BRUSH	
	☐VACUUM ☐BRUSH	
	☐VACUUM ☐BRUSH	
	☐VACUUM ☐BRUSH	
	☐VACUUM ☐BRUSH	
	☐VACUUM ☐BRUSH	
	☐VACUUM ☐BRUSH	
	☐VACUUM ☐BRUSH	
	☐VACUUM ☐BRUSH	
	☐VACUUM ☐BRUSH	
	☐VACUUM ☐BRUSH	
	☐VACUUM ☐BRUSH	
	☐VACUUM ☐BRUSH	
	☐VACUUM ☐BRUSH	
	☐VACUUM ☐BRUSH	
	☐VACUUM ☐BRUSH	
	☐VACUUM ☐BRUSH	
	☐VACUUM ☐BRUSH	
	☐VACUUM ☐BRUSH	
	☐VACUUM ☐BRUSH	
	☐VACUUM ☐BRUSH	

POOL MAINTENANCE LOG

MAINTENANCE		
BACKWASH	**VACUUM AND/OR BRUSH**	**CONTAMINANT EPISODE**
	☐ VACUUM ☐ BRUSH	
	☐ VACUUM ☐ BRUSH	
	☐ VACUUM ☐ BRUSH	
	☐ VACUUM ☐ BRUSH	
	☐ VACUUM ☐ BRUSH	
	☐ VACUUM ☐ BRUSH	
	☐ VACUUM ☐ BRUSH	
	☐ VACUUM ☐ BRUSH	
	☐ VACUUM ☐ BRUSH	
	☐ VACUUM ☐ BRUSH	
	☐ VACUUM ☐ BRUSH	
	☐ VACUUM ☐ BRUSH	
	☐ VACUUM ☐ BRUSH	
	☐ VACUUM ☐ BRUSH	
	☐ VACUUM ☐ BRUSH	
	☐ VACUUM ☐ BRUSH	
	☐ VACUUM ☐ BRUSH	
	☐ VACUUM ☐ BRUSH	
	☐ VACUUM ☐ BRUSH	
	☐ VACUUM ☐ BRUSH	
	☐ VACUUM ☐ BRUSH	
	☐ VACUUM ☐ BRUSH	
	☐ VACUUM ☐ BRUSH	
	☐ VACUUM ☐ BRUSH	
	☐ VACUUM ☐ BRUSH	
	☐ VACUUM ☐ BRUSH	
	☐ VACUUM ☐ BRUSH	

MAINTENANCE LOG

DATE		TIME		LAST CHECK	

POOL ID	

CHECKLIST	CHECKED?	VALUE / REMARK
CHECK FILTERS	☐YES ☐NO	
CHECK PUMPS	☐YES ☐NOO	
CHECK WATER TEMPERATURE	☐YES ☐NO	WATER TEMPERATURE:
CHECK WATER LEVEL	☐YES ☐NO	WATER LEVEL:
CHECK WATER FLOW RATE	☐YES ☐NO	WATER FLOW RATE:
WATER PH LEVEL (IDEAL 7.4 - 7.6)	☐YES ☐NO	PH LEVEL:
WATER CHLORINE LEVEL	☐YES ☐NOO	CHLORINE LEVEL:
CHECK OVERALL WATER CLARITY	☐YES ☐NO	
CHECK SKIMMER BASKETS	☐YES ☐NO	
LEAF SKIMMING	☐YES ☐NO	
BRUSH SIDES	☐YES ☐NO	
VACUUM POOL	☐YES ☐NOO	
CHECK CHEMICAL STOCK LEVEL	☐YES ☐NO	ITEMS TO PURCHASE:
CHECK FIRST AID SUPPLIES	☐YES ☐NO	ITEMS NEEDED:
SURROUNDING STRUCTURES CHECK	☐YES ☐NO	CONDITION

CHECKED BY:		SIGNATURE	

MAINTENANCE LOG

DATE		TIME		LAST CHECK	

POOL ID

CHECKLIST	CHECKED?	VALUE / REMARK
CHECK FILTERS	☐YES ☐NO	
CHECK PUMPS	☐YES ☐NOO	
CHECK WATER TEMPERATURE	☐YES ☐NO	WATER TEMPERATURE:
CHECK WATER LEVEL	☐YES ☐NO	WATER LEVEL:
CHECK WATER FLOW RATE	☐YES ☐NO	WATER FLOW RATE:
WATER PH LEVEL (IDEAL 7.4 - 7.6)	☐YES ☐NO	PH LEVEL:
WATER CHLORINE LEVEL	☐YES ☐NOO	CHLORINE LEVEL:
CHECK OVERALL WATER CLARITY	☐YES ☐NO	
CHECK SKIMMER BASKETS	☐YES ☐NO	
LEAF SKIMMING	☐YES ☐NO	
BRUSH SIDES	☐YES ☐NO	
VACUUM POOL	☐YES ☐NOO	
CHECK CHEMICAL STOCK LEVEL	☐YES ☐NO	ITEMS TO PURCHASE:
CHECK FIRST AID SUPPLIES	☐YES ☐NO	ITEMS NEEDED:
SURROUNDING STRUCTURES CHECK	☐YES ☐NO	CONDITION

CHECKED BY:		SIGNATURE	

SUPPLIES REORDER LIST

DATE		

ITEM	STOCK NUMBER

SUPPLIES REORDER LIST

DATE		

ITEM	STOCK NUMBER

SPA INFORMATION RECORD

SPA NAME			
MODEL			
PURCHASE DATE		SERIAL #	
WARRANTY LENGTH		VOLTAGE	☐110 V ☐220 V
GALLONS		OZONATOR	☐YES ☐NO
COVER SIZE		FILTER NUMBER	

FILTER MAINTENANCE RECORD
CLEAN EVERY 3-4 MONTHS, AND WITH EACH WATER CHARGE. REPLACE ANNUALLY.

DATE		CLEANED	REPLACED
		☐	☐
		☐	☐
		☐	☐
		☐	☐
		☐	☐
		☐	☐
		☐	☐

REPAIR RECORD

DATE	DETAILS

SPA INFORMATION RECORD

SPA NAME	
MODEL	

PURCHASE DATE		SERIAL #	
WARRANTY LENGTH		VOLTAGE	☐110 V ☐220 V
GALLONS		OZONATOR	☐YES ☐NO
COVER SIZE		FILTER NUMBER	

FILTER MAINTENANCE RECORD
CLEAN EVERY 3-4 MONTHS, AND WITH EACH WATER CHARGE. REPLACE ANNUALLY.

DATE		CLEANED	REPLACED
		☐	☐
		☐	☐
		☐	☐
		☐	☐
		☐	☐
		☐	☐
		☐	☐

REPAIR RECORD

DATE	DETAILS

SPA RECORD

DATE

	FACTOR	INITIAL READING	PRODUCT ADDED	FINAL READING	AMOUNT ADDED
WATER CHARGED ☐	TA				
	PH				
FILTER CHANGED ☐	HARDNESS				
	SANITIZER				
FILTER REPLACED ☐	SHOCK				
	CLARIFIER				
	METAL REDUCER				
5					

NOTES

DATE

	FACTOR	INITIAL READING	PRODUCT ADDED	FINAL READING	AMOUNT ADDED
WATER CHARGED ☐	TA				
	PH				
FILTER CHANGED ☐	HARDNESS				
	SANITIZER				
FILTER REPLACED ☐	SHOCK				
	CLARIFIER				
	METAL REDUCER				
5					

NOTES

SPA RECORD

DATE

	FACTOR	INITIAL READING	PRODUCT ADDED	FINAL READING	AMOUNT ADDED
WATER CHARGED ☐	TA				
	PH				
FILTER CHANGED ☐	HARDNESS				
	SANITIZER				
FILTER REPLACED ☐	SHOCK				
	CLARIFIER				
	METAL REDUCER				
5					

NOTES

DATE

	FACTOR	INITIAL READING	PRODUCT ADDED	FINAL READING	AMOUNT ADDED
WATER CHARGED ☐	TA				
	PH				
FILTER CHANGED ☐	HARDNESS				
	SANITIZER				
FILTER REPLACED ☐	SHOCK				
	CLARIFIER				
	METAL REDUCER				
5					

NOTES

POOL / SPA DAILY MAINTENANCE

FACILITY NAME	
FACILITY ADDRESS	

MINIMUM TURNOVER RATE (GPM)		MONTH & YEAR	

DATE	CHLORINE RESIDUAL (FREE CHLORINE)	PH	CHEMICALS ADDED (TYPE AND AMOUNT)	TEMP (°F)	OTHER MAINTENANCE (BACKWASH ETC.)
1					
2					
3					
4					
5					
6					
7					
8					
9					
10					
11					
12					
13					
14					
15					
16					
17					
18					
19					
20					
21					
22					
23					
24					
25					
26					
27					
28					
29					
30					
31					

POOL / SPA DAILY MAINTENANCE

FACILITY NAME	
FACILITY ADDRESS	
MINIMUM TURNOVER RATE (GPM)		MONTH & YEAR	

DATE	CHLORINE RESIDUAL (FREE CHLORINE)	PH	CHEMICALS ADDED (TYPE AND AMOUNT)	TEMP (°F)	OTHER MAINTENANCE (BACKWASH ETC.)
1					
2					
3					
4					
5					
6					
7					
8					
9					
10					
11					
12					
13					
14					
15					
16					
17					
18					
19					
20					
21					
22					
23					
24					
25					
26					
27					
28					
29					
30					
31					

POOL MAINTENANCE LOG

POOL/CLIENT NAME		DATE	
LOCATION		POOL SIZE	
FLOW RATE REQUIRED		DISINFECTANT TYPE	

DAILY TEST	TIME (AM/PM)						
	WATER CLARITY						
	DISINFECTANT PPM						
	COMBINED CHLORINE <50% FREE						
	PH 7.2-8.0						
	FLOW GPM						

WEEKLY TEST	ALKALINITY REC RANGE 60-160 PPM						
	CYANURIC ACID IF USED - < 90						

CHEMICALS ADDED	QTY OF DISINFECTANT ADDED						
	OTHER CHEMICALS ADDED						

POOL MAINTENANCE LOG

POOL/CLIENT NAME		DATE	
LOCATION		POOL SIZE	
FLOW RATE REQUIRED		DISINFECTANT TYPE	

DAILY TEST	TIME (AM/PM)						
	WATER CLARITY						
	DISINFECTANT PPM						
	COMBINED CHLORINE <50% FREE						
	PH 7.2-8.0						
	FLOW GPM						

WEEKLY TEST	ALKALINITY REC RANGE 60-160 PPM						
	CYANURIC ACID IF USED - < 90						

CHEMICALS ADDED	QTY OF DISINFECTANT ADDED						
	OTHER CHEMICALS ADDED						

POOL MAINTENANCE LOG

	MAINTENANCE	
BACKWASH	**VACUUM AND/OR BRUSH**	**CONTAMINANT EPISODE**
	☐VACUUM ☐BRUSH	
	☐VACUUM ☐BRUSH	
	☐VACUUM ☐BRUSH	
	☐VACUUM ☐BRUSH	
	☐VACUUM ☐BRUSH	
	☐VACUUM ☐BRUSH	
	☐VACUUM ☐BRUSH	
	☐VACUUM ☐BRUSH	
	☐VACUUM ☐BRUSH	
	☐VACUUM ☐BRUSH	
	☐VACUUM ☐BRUSH	
	☐VACUUM ☐BRUSH	
	☐VACUUM ☐BRUSH	
	☐VACUUM ☐BRUSH	
	☐VACUUM ☐BRUSH	
	☐VACUUM ☐BRUSH	
	☐VACUUM ☐BRUSH	
	☐VACUUM ☐BRUSH	
	☐VACUUM ☐BRUSH	
	☐VACUUM ☐BRUSH	
	☐VACUUM ☐BRUSH	
	☐VACUUM ☐BRUSH	
	☐VACUUM ☐BRUSH	
	☐VACUUM ☐BRUSH	
	☐VACUUM ☐BRUSH	
	☐VACUUM ☐BRUSH	
	☐VACUUM ☐BRUSH	

POOL MAINTENANCE LOG

MAINTENANCE		
BACKWASH	VACUUM AND/OR BRUSH	CONTAMINANT EPISODE
	☐VACUUM ☐BRUSH	
	☐VACUUM ☐BRUSH	
	☐VACUUM ☐BRUSH	
	☐VACUUM ☐BRUSH	
	☐VACUUM ☐BRUSH	
	☐VACUUM ☐BRUSH	
	☐VACUUM ☐BRUSH	
	☐VACUUM ☐BRUSH	
	☐VACUUM ☐BRUSH	
	☐VACUUM ☐BRUSH	
	☐VACUUM ☐BRUSH	
	☐VACUUM ☐BRUSH	
	☐VACUUM ☐BRUSH	
	☐VACUUM ☐BRUSH	
	☐VACUUM ☐BRUSH	
	☐VACUUM ☐BRUSH	
	☐VACUUM ☐BRUSH	
	☐VACUUM ☐BRUSH	
	☐VACUUM ☐BRUSH	
	☐VACUUM ☐BRUSH	
	☐VACUUM ☐BRUSH	
	☐VACUUM ☐BRUSH	
	☐VACUUM ☐BRUSH	
	☐VACUUM ☐BRUSH	
	☐VACUUM ☐BRUSH	
	☐VACUUM ☐BRUSH	
	☐VACUUM ☐BRUSH	

MAINTENANCE LOG

DATE		TIME		LAST CHECK	

POOL ID	

CHECKLIST	CHECKED?	VALUE / REMARK
CHECK FILTERS	☐YES ☐NO	
CHECK PUMPS	☐YES ☐NOO	
CHECK WATER TEMPERATURE	☐YES ☐NO	WATER TEMPERATURE:
CHECK WATER LEVEL	☐YES ☐NO	WATER LEVEL:
CHECK WATER FLOW RATE	☐YES ☐NO	WATER FLOW RATE:
WATER PH LEVEL (IDEAL 7.4 - 7.6)	☐YES ☐NO	PH LEVEL:
WATER CHLORINE LEVEL	☐YES ☐NOO	CHLORINE LEVEL:
CHECK OVERALL WATER CLARITY	☐YES ☐NO	
CHECK SKIMMER BASKETS	☐YES ☐NO	
LEAF SKIMMING	☐YES ☐NO	
BRUSH SIDES	☐YES ☐NO	
VACUUM POOL	☐YES ☐NOO	
CHECK CHEMICAL STOCK LEVEL	☐YES ☐NO	ITEMS TO PURCHASE:
CHECK FIRST AID SUPPLIES	☐YES ☐NO	ITEMS NEEDED:
SURROUNDING STRUCTURES CHECK	☐YES ☐NO	CONDITION

CHECKED BY:		SIGNATURE	

MAINTENANCE LOG

DATE		TIME		LAST CHECK	

POOL ID	

CHECKLIST	CHECKED?	VALUE / REMARK
CHECK FILTERS	☐YES ☐NO	
CHECK PUMPS	☐YES ☐NOO	
CHECK WATER TEMPERATURE	☐YES ☐NO	WATER TEMPERATURE:
CHECK WATER LEVEL	☐YES ☐NO	WATER LEVEL:
CHECK WATER FLOW RATE	☐YES ☐NO	WATER FLOW RATE:
WATER PH LEVEL (IDEAL 7.4 - 7.6)	☐YES ☐NO	PH LEVEL:
WATER CHLORINE LEVEL	☐YES ☐NOO	CHLORINE LEVEL:
CHECK OVERALL WATER CLARITY	☐YES ☐NO	
CHECK SKIMMER BASKETS	☐YES ☐NO	
LEAF SKIMMING	☐YES ☐NO	
BRUSH SIDES	☐YES ☐NO	
VACUUM POOL	☐YES ☐NOO	
CHECK CHEMICAL STOCK LEVEL	☐YES ☐NO	ITEMS TO PURCHASE:
CHECK FIRST AID SUPPLIES	☐YES ☐NO	ITEMS NEEDED:
SURROUNDING STRUCTURES CHECK	☐YES ☐NO	CONDITION

CHECKED BY:		SIGNATURE	

SUPPLIES REORDER LIST

DATE		

ITEM	STOCK NUMBER

SUPPLIES REORDER LIST

DATE		

ITEM	STOCK NUMBER

SPA INFORMATION RECORD

SPA NAME	
MODEL	

PURCHASE DATE		SERIAL #	
WARRANTY LENGTH		VOLTAGE	☐110 V ☐220 V
GALLONS		OZONATOR	☐YES ☐NO
COVER SIZE		FILTER NUMBER	

FILTER MAINTENANCE RECORD
CLEAN EVERY 3-4 MONTHS, AND WITH EACH WATER CHARGE. REPLACE ANNUALLY.

DATE		CLEANED	REPLACED
		☐	☐
		☐	☐
		☐	☐
		☐	☐
		☐	☐
		☐	☐
		☐	☐

REPAIR RECORD

DATE	DETAILS

SPA INFORMATION RECORD

SPA NAME			
MODEL			
PURCHASE DATE		SERIAL #	
WARRANTY LENGTH		VOLTAGE	☐ 110 V ☐ 220 V
GALLONS		OZONATOR	☐ YES ☐ NO
COVER SIZE		FILTER NUMBER	

FILTER MAINTENANCE RECORD
CLEAN EVERY 3-4 MONTHS, AND WITH EACH WATER CHARGE. REPLACE ANNUALLY.

DATE		CLEANED	REPLACED
		☐	☐
		☐	☐
		☐	☐
		☐	☐
		☐	☐
		☐	☐
		☐	☐

REPAIR RECORD

DATE	DETAILS

SPA RECORD

DATE

	FACTOR	INITIAL READING	PRODUCT ADDED	FINAL READING	AMOUNT ADDED
WATER CHARGED ☐	TA				
	PH				
FILTER CHANGED ☐	HARDNESS				
	SANITIZER				
FILTER REPLACED ☐	SHOCK				
	CLARIFIER				
	METAL REDUCER				
5					

NOTES

DATE

	FACTOR	INITIAL READING	PRODUCT ADDED	FINAL READING	AMOUNT ADDED
WATER CHARGED ☐	TA				
	PH				
FILTER CHANGED ☐	HARDNESS				
	SANITIZER				
FILTER REPLACED ☐	SHOCK				
	CLARIFIER				
	METAL REDUCER				
5					

NOTES

SPA RECORD

DATE

	FACTOR	INITIAL READING	PRODUCT ADDED	FINAL READING	AMOUNT ADDED
WATER CHARGED ☐	TA				
	PH				
FILTER CHANGED ☐	HARDNESS				
	SANITIZER				
FILTER REPLACED ☐	SHOCK				
	CLARIFIER				
5	METAL REDUCER				

NOTES

DATE

	FACTOR	INITIAL READING	PRODUCT ADDED	FINAL READING	AMOUNT ADDED
WATER CHARGED ☐	TA				
	PH				
FILTER CHANGED ☐	HARDNESS				
	SANITIZER				
FILTER REPLACED ☐	SHOCK				
	CLARIFIER				
5	METAL REDUCER				

NOTES

POOL / SPA DAILY MAINTENANCE

FACILITY NAME					
FACILITY ADDRESS					
MINIMUM TURNOVER RATE (GPM)				MONTH & YEAR	

DATE	CHLORINE RESIDUAL (FREE CHLORINE)	PH	CHEMICALS ADDED (TYPE AND AMOUNT)	TEMP (°F)	OTHER MAINTENANCE (BACKWASH ETC.)
1					
2					
3					
4					
5					
6					
7					
8					
9					
10					
11					
12					
13					
14					
15					
16					
17					
18					
19					
20					
21					
22					
23					
24					
25					
26					
27					
28					
29					
30					
31					

POOL / SPA DAILY MAINTENANCE

FACILITY NAME	
FACILITY ADDRESS	

MINIMUM TURNOVER RATE (GPM)		MONTH & YEAR	

DATE	CHLORINE RESIDUAL (FREE CHLORINE)	PH	CHEMICALS ADDED (TYPE AND AMOUNT)	TEMP (°F)	OTHER MAINTENANCE (BACKWASH ETC.)
1					
2					
3					
4					
5					
6					
7					
8					
9					
10					
11					
12					
13					
14					
15					
16					
17					
18					
19					
20					
21					
22					
23					
24					
25					
26					
27					
28					
29					
30					
31					

POOL MAINTENANCE LOG

POOL/CLIENT NAME		DATE	
LOCATION		POOL SIZE	
FLOW RATE REQUIRED		DISINFECTANT TYPE	

DAILY TEST						
	TIME (AM/PM)					
	WATER CLARITY					
	DISINFECTANT PPM					
	COMBINED CHLORINE <50% FREE					
	PH 7.2-8.0					
	FLOW GPM					

WEEKLY TEST						
	ALKALINITY REC RANGE 60-160 PPM					
	CYANURIC ACID IF USED - < 90					

CHEMICALS ADDED						
	QTY OF DISINFECTANT ADDED					
	OTHER CHEMICALS ADDED					

POOL MAINTENANCE LOG

POOL/CLIENT NAME		DATE	
LOCATION		POOL SIZE	
FLOW RATE REQUIRED		DISINFECTANT TYPE	

DAILY TEST	TIME (AM/PM)					
	WATER CLARITY					
	DISINFECTANT PPM					
	COMBINED CHLORINE <50% FREE					
	PH 7.2-8.0					
	FLOW GPM					

WEEKLY TEST	ALKALINITY REC RANGE 60-160 PPM					
	CYANURIC ACID IF USED - < 90					

CHEMICALS ADDED	QTY OF DISINFECTANT ADDED					
	OTHER CHEMICALS ADDED					

POOL MAINTENANCE LOG

MAINTENANCE		
BACKWASH	VACUUM AND/OR BRUSH	CONTAMINANT EPISODE
	☐VACUUM ☐BRUSH	
	☐VACUUM ☐BRUSH	
	☐VACUUM ☐BRUSH	
	☐VACUUM ☐BRUSH	
	☐VACUUM ☐BRUSH	
	☐VACUUM ☐BRUSH	
	☐VACUUM ☐BRUSH	
	☐VACUUM ☐BRUSH	
	☐VACUUM ☐BRUSH	
	☐VACUUM ☐BRUSH	
	☐VACUUM ☐BRUSH	
	☐VACUUM ☐BRUSH	
	☐VACUUM ☐BRUSH	
	☐VACUUM ☐BRUSH	
	☐VACUUM ☐BRUSH	
	☐VACUUM ☐BRUSH	
	☐VACUUM ☐BRUSH	
	☐VACUUM ☐BRUSH	
	☐VACUUM ☐BRUSH	
	☐VACUUM ☐BRUSH	
	☐VACUUM ☐BRUSH	
	☐VACUUM ☐BRUSH	
	☐VACUUM ☐BRUSH	
	☐VACUUM ☐BRUSH	
	☐VACUUM ☐BRUSH	
	☐VACUUM ☐BRUSH	
	☐VACUUM ☐BRUSH	

POOL MAINTENANCE LOG

	MAINTENANCE	
BACKWASH	VACUUM AND/OR BRUSH	CONTAMINANT EPISODE
	☐VACUUM ☐BRUSH	
	☐VACUUM ☐BRUSH	
	☐VACUUM ☐BRUSH	
	☐VACUUM ☐BRUSH	
	☐VACUUM ☐BRUSH	
	☐VACUUM ☐BRUSH	
	☐VACUUM ☐BRUSH	
	☐VACUUM ☐BRUSH	
	☐VACUUM ☐BRUSH	
	☐VACUUM ☐BRUSH	
	☐VACUUM ☐BRUSH	
	☐VACUUM ☐BRUSH	
	☐VACUUM ☐BRUSH	
	☐VACUUM ☐BRUSH	
	☐VACUUM ☐BRUSH	
	☐VACUUM ☐BRUSH	
	☐VACUUM ☐BRUSH	
	☐VACUUM ☐BRUSH	
	☐VACUUM ☐BRUSH	
	☐VACUUM ☐BRUSH	
	☐VACUUM ☐BRUSH	
	☐VACUUM ☐BRUSH	
	☐VACUUM ☐BRUSH	
	☐VACUUM ☐BRUSH	
	☐VACUUM ☐BRUSH	
	☐VACUUM ☐BRUSH	

MAINTENANCE LOG

DATE		TIME		LAST CHECK	

POOL ID	

CHECKLIST	CHECKED?	VALUE / REMARK
CHECK FILTERS	☐YES ☐NO	
CHECK PUMPS	☐YES ☐NOO	
CHECK WATER TEMPERATURE	☐YES ☐NO	WATER TEMPERATURE:
CHECK WATER LEVEL	☐YES ☐NO	WATER LEVEL:
CHECK WATER FLOW RATE	☐YES ☐NO	WATER FLOW RATE:
WATER PH LEVEL (IDEAL 7.4 - 7.6)	☐YES ☐NO	PH LEVEL:
WATER CHLORINE LEVEL	☐YES ☐NOO	CHLORINE LEVEL:
CHECK OVERALL WATER CLARITY	☐YES ☐NO	
CHECK SKIMMER BASKETS	☐YES ☐NO	
LEAF SKIMMING	☐YES ☐NO	
BRUSH SIDES	☐YES ☐NO	
VACUUM POOL	☐YES ☐NOO	
CHECK CHEMICAL STOCK LEVEL	☐YES ☐NO	ITEMS TO PURCHASE:
CHECK FIRST AID SUPPLIES	☐YES ☐NO	ITEMS NEEDED:
SURROUNDING STRUCTURES CHECK	☐YES ☐NO	CONDITION

CHECKED BY:		SIGNATURE	

MAINTENANCE LOG

DATE		TIME		LAST CHECK	

POOL ID	

CHECKLIST	CHECKED?	VALUE / REMARK
CHECK FILTERS	☐YES ☐NO	
CHECK PUMPS	☐YES ☐NOO	
CHECK WATER TEMPERATURE	☐YES ☐NO	WATER TEMPERATURE:
CHECK WATER LEVEL	☐YES ☐NO	WATER LEVEL:
CHECK WATER FLOW RATE	☐YES ☐NO	WATER FLOW RATE:
WATER PH LEVEL (IDEAL 7.4 - 7.6)	☐YES ☐NO	PH LEVEL:
WATER CHLORINE LEVEL	☐YES ☐NOO	CHLORINE LEVEL:
CHECK OVERALL WATER CLARITY	☐YES ☐NO	
CHECK SKIMMER BASKETS	☐YES ☐NO	
LEAF SKIMMING	☐YES ☐NO	
BRUSH SIDES	☐YES ☐NO	
VACUUM POOL	☐YES ☐NOO	
CHECK CHEMICAL STOCK LEVEL	☐YES ☐NO	ITEMS TO PURCHASE:
CHECK FIRST AID SUPPLIES	☐YES ☐NO	ITEMS NEEDED:
SURROUNDING STRUCTURES CHECK	☐YES ☐NO	CONDITION

CHECKED BY:		SIGNATURE	

SUPPLIES REORDER LIST

DATE		

ITEM	STOCK NUMBER

SUPPLIES REORDER LIST

DATE		

ITEM	STOCK NUMBER

SPA INFORMATION RECORD

SPA NAME	
MODEL	
PURCHASE DATE	
WARRANTY LENGTH	
GALLONS	
COVER SIZE	

SERIAL #	
VOLTAGE	☐110 V ☐220 V
OZONATOR	☐YES ☐NO
FILTER NUMBER	

FILTER MAINTENANCE RECORD
CLEAN EVERY 3-4 MONTHS, AND WITH EACH WATER CHARGE. REPLACE ANNUALLY.

DATE		CLEANED	REPLACED
		☐	☐
		☐	☐
		☐	☐
		☐	☐
		☐	☐
		☐	☐
		☐	☐

REPAIR RECORD

DATE	DETAILS

SPA INFORMATION RECORD

SPA NAME	
MODEL	

PURCHASE DATE		SERIAL #	
WARRANTY LENGTH		VOLTAGE	☐110 V ☐220 V
GALLONS		OZONATOR	☐YES ☐NO
COVER SIZE		FILTER NUMBER	

FILTER MAINTENANCE RECORD
CLEAN EVERY 3-4 MONTHS, AND WITH EACH WATER CHARGE. REPLACE ANNUALLY.

DATE		CLEANED	REPLACED
		☐	☐
		☐	☐
		☐	☐
		☐	☐
		☐	☐
		☐	☐
		☐	☐

REPAIR RECORD

DATE	DETAILS

SPA RECORD

	FACTOR	INITIAL READING	PRODUCT ADDED	FINAL READING	AMOUNT ADDED
WATER CHARGED ☐	TA				
	PH				
FILTER CHANGED ☐	HARDNESS				
	SANITIZER				
FILTER REPLACED ☐	SHOCK				
	CLARIFIER				
	METAL REDUCER				
5					

NOTES

DATE

	FACTOR	INITIAL READING	PRODUCT ADDED	FINAL READING	AMOUNT ADDED
WATER CHARGED ☐	TA				
	PH				
FILTER CHANGED ☐	HARDNESS				
	SANITIZER				
FILTER REPLACED ☐	SHOCK				
	CLARIFIER				
	METAL REDUCER				
5					

NOTES

SPA RECORD

DATE

	FACTOR	INITIAL READING	PRODUCT ADDED	FINAL READING	AMOUNT ADDED
WATER CHARGED ☐	TA				
	PH				
FILTER CHANGED ☐	HARDNESS				
	SANITIZER				
FILTER REPLACED ☐	SHOCK				
	CLARIFIER				
5	METAL REDUCER				

NOTES

DATE

	FACTOR	INITIAL READING	PRODUCT ADDED	FINAL READING	AMOUNT ADDED
WATER CHARGED ☐	TA				
	PH				
FILTER CHANGED ☐	HARDNESS				
	SANITIZER				
FILTER REPLACED ☐	SHOCK				
	CLARIFIER				
5	METAL REDUCER				

NOTES

POOL / SPA DAILY MAINTENANCE

FACILITY NAME	
FACILITY ADDRESS	

MINIMUM TURNOVER RATE (GPM)		MONTH & YEAR	

DATE	CHLORINE RESIDUAL (FREE CHLORINE)	PH	CHEMICALS ADDED (TYPE AND AMOUNT)	TEMP (°F)	OTHER MAINTENANCE (BACKWASH ETC.)
1					
2					
3					
4					
5					
6					
7					
8					
9					
10					
11					
12					
13					
14					
15					
16					
17					
18					
19					
20					
21					
22					
23					
24					
25					
26					
27					
28					
29					
30					
31					

POOL / SPA DAILY MAINTENANCE

FACILITY NAME	
FACILITY ADDRESS	

MINIMUM TURNOVER RATE (GPM)		MONTH & YEAR	

DATE	CHLORINE RESIDUAL (FREE CHLORINE)	PH	CHEMICALS ADDED (TYPE AND AMOUNT)	TEMP (°F)	OTHER MAINTENANCE (BACKWASH ETC.)
1					
2					
3					
4					
5					
6					
7					
8					
9					
10					
11					
12					
13					
14					
15					
16					
17					
18					
19					
20					
21					
22					
23					
24					
25					
26					
27					
28					
29					
30					
31					

POOL MAINTENANCE LOG

POOL/CLIENT NAME		DATE	
LOCATION		POOL SIZE	
FLOW RATE REQUIRED		DISINFECTANT TYPE	

DAILY TEST						
	TIME (AM/PM)					
	WATER CLARITY					
	DISINFECTANT PPM					
	COMBINED CHLORINE <50% FREE					
	PH 7.2-8.0					
	FLOW GPM					

WEEKLY TEST						
	ALKALINITY REC RANGE 60-160 PPM					
	CYANURIC ACID IF USED - < 90					

CHEMICALS ADDED						
	QTY OF DISINFECTANT ADDED					
	OTHER CHEMICALS ADDED					

POOL MAINTENANCE LOG

POOL/CLIENT NAME		DATE	
LOCATION		POOL SIZE	
FLOW RATE REQUIRED		DISINFECTANT TYPE	

DAILY TEST	TIME (AM/PM)						
	WATER CLARITY						
	DISINFECTANT PPM						
	COMBINED CHLORINE <50% FREE						
	PH 7.2-8.0						
	FLOW GPM						

WEEKLY TEST	ALKALINITY REC RANGE 60-160 PPM						
	CYANURIC ACID IF USED - < 90						

CHEMICALS ADDED	QTY OF DISINFECTANT ADDED						
	OTHER CHEMICALS ADDED						

POOL MAINTENANCE LOG

MAINTENANCE		
BACKWASH	VACUUM AND/OR BRUSH	CONTAMINANT EPISODE
	☐VACUUM ☐BRUSH	
	☐VACUUM ☐BRUSH	
	☐VACUUM ☐BRUSH	
	☐VACUUM ☐BRUSH	
	☐VACUUM ☐BRUSH	
	☐VACUUM ☐BRUSH	
	☐VACUUM ☐BRUSH	
	☐VACUUM ☐BRUSH	
	☐VACUUM ☐BRUSH	
	☐VACUUM ☐BRUSH	
	☐VACUUM ☐BRUSH	
	☐VACUUM ☐BRUSH	
	☐VACUUM ☐BRUSH	
	☐VACUUM ☐BRUSH	
	☐VACUUM ☐BRUSH	
	☐VACUUM ☐BRUSH	
	☐VACUUM ☐BRUSH	
	☐VACUUM ☐BRUSH	
	☐VACUUM ☐BRUSH	
	☐VACUUM ☐BRUSH	
	☐VACUUM ☐BRUSH	
	☐VACUUM ☐BRUSH	
	☐VACUUM ☐BRUSH	
	☐VACUUM ☐BRUSH	
	☐VACUUM ☐BRUSH	
	☐VACUUM ☐BRUSH	

POOL MAINTENANCE LOG

MAINTENANCE		
BACKWASH	VACUUM AND/OR BRUSH	CONTAMINANT EPISODE
	☐VACUUM ☐BRUSH	
	☐VACUUM ☐BRUSH	
	☐VACUUM ☐BRUSH	
	☐VACUUM ☐BRUSH	
	☐VACUUM ☐BRUSH	
	☐VACUUM ☐BRUSH	
	☐VACUUM ☐BRUSH	
	☐VACUUM ☐BRUSH	
	☐VACUUM ☐BRUSH	
	☐VACUUM ☐BRUSH	
	☐VACUUM ☐BRUSH	
	☐VACUUM ☐BRUSH	
	☐VACUUM ☐BRUSH	
	☐VACUUM ☐BRUSH	
	☐VACUUM ☐BRUSH	
	☐VACUUM ☐BRUSH	
	☐VACUUM ☐BRUSH	
	☐VACUUM ☐BRUSH	
	☐VACUUM ☐BRUSH	
	☐VACUUM ☐BRUSH	
	☐VACUUM ☐BRUSH	
	☐VACUUM ☐BRUSH	
	☐VACUUM ☐BRUSH	
	☐VACUUM ☐BRUSH	
	☐VACUUM ☐BRUSH	
	☐VACUUM ☐BRUSH	
	☐VACUUM ☐BRUSH	

MAINTENANCE LOG

DATE		TIME		LAST CHECK	

POOL ID	

CHECKLIST	CHECKED?	VALUE / REMARK
CHECK FILTERS	☐YES ☐NO	
CHECK PUMPS	☐YES ☐NOO	
CHECK WATER TEMPERATURE	☐YES ☐NO	WATER TEMPERATURE:
CHECK WATER LEVEL	☐YES ☐NO	WATER LEVEL:
CHECK WATER FLOW RATE	☐YES ☐NO	WATER FLOW RATE:
WATER PH LEVEL (IDEAL 7.4 - 7.6)	☐YES ☐NO	PH LEVEL:
WATER CHLORINE LEVEL	☐YES ☐NOO	CHLORINE LEVEL:
CHECK OVERALL WATER CLARITY	☐YES ☐NO	
CHECK SKIMMER BASKETS	☐YES ☐NO	
LEAF SKIMMING	☐YES ☐NO	
BRUSH SIDES	☐YES ☐NO	
VACUUM POOL	☐YES ☐NOO	
CHECK CHEMICAL STOCK LEVEL	☐YES ☐NO	ITEMS TO PURCHASE:
CHECK FIRST AID SUPPLIES	☐YES ☐NO	ITEMS NEEDED:
SURROUNDING STRUCTURES CHECK	☐YES ☐NO	CONDITION

CHECKED BY:		SIGNATURE	

MAINTENANCE LOG

DATE		TIME		LAST CHECK	

POOL ID

CHECKLIST	CHECKED?	VALUE / REMARK
CHECK FILTERS	☐YES ☐NO	
CHECK PUMPS	☐YES ☐NOO	
CHECK WATER TEMPERATURE	☐YES ☐NO	WATER TEMPERATURE:
CHECK WATER LEVEL	☐YES ☐NO	WATER LEVEL:
CHECK WATER FLOW RATE	☐YES ☐NO	WATER FLOW RATE:
WATER PH LEVEL (IDEAL 7.4 - 7.6)	☐YES ☐NO	PH LEVEL:
WATER CHLORINE LEVEL	☐YES ☐NOO	CHLORINE LEVEL:
CHECK OVERALL WATER CLARITY	☐YES ☐NO	
CHECK SKIMMER BASKETS	☐YES ☐NO	
LEAF SKIMMING	☐YES ☐NO	
BRUSH SIDES	☐YES ☐NO	
VACUUM POOL	☐YES ☐NOO	
CHECK CHEMICAL STOCK LEVEL	☐YES ☐NO	ITEMS TO PURCHASE:
CHECK FIRST AID SUPPLIES	☐YES ☐NO	ITEMS NEEDED:
SURROUNDING STRUCTURES CHECK	☐YES ☐NO	CONDITION

CHECKED BY:		SIGNATURE	

SUPPLIES REORDER LIST

DATE		

ITEM	STOCK NUMBER

SUPPLIES REORDER LIST

DATE	

ITEM	STOCK NUMBER

SPA INFORMATION RECORD

SPA NAME				
MODEL				
PURCHASE DATE		**SERIAL #**		
WARRANTY LENGTH		**VOLTAGE**	☐110 V ☐220 V	
GALLONS		**OZONATOR**	☐YES ☐NO	
COVER SIZE		**FILTER NUMBER**		

FILTER MAINTENANCE RECORD
CLEAN EVERY 3-4 MONTHS, AND WITH EACH WATER CHARGE. REPLACE ANNUALLY.

DATE		CLEANED	REPLACED
		☐	☐
		☐	☐
		☐	☐
		☐	☐
		☐	☐
		☐	☐
		☐	☐

REPAIR RECORD

DATE	DETAILS

SPA INFORMATION RECORD

SPA NAME	
MODEL	

PURCHASE DATE		SERIAL #	
WARRANTY LENGTH		VOLTAGE	☐110 V ☐220 V
GALLONS		OZONATOR	☐YES ☐NO
COVER SIZE		FILTER NUMBER	

FILTER MAINTENANCE RECORD
CLEAN EVERY 3-4 MONTHS, AND WITH EACH WATER CHARGE. REPLACE ANNUALLY.

DATE		CLEANED	REPLACED
		☐	☐
		☐	☐
		☐	☐
		☐	☐
		☐	☐
		☐	☐
		☐	☐

REPAIR RECORD

DATE	DETAILS

SPA RECORD

DATE

	FACTOR	INITIAL READING	PRODUCT ADDED	FINAL READING	AMOUNT ADDED
WATER CHARGED ☐	TA				
	PH				
FILTER CHANGED ☐	HARDNESS				
	SANITIZER				
FILTER REPLACED ☐	SHOCK				
	CLARIFIER				
	METAL REDUCER				
5					

NOTES

DATE

	FACTOR	INITIAL READING	PRODUCT ADDED	FINAL READING	AMOUNT ADDED
WATER CHARGED ☐	TA				
	PH				
FILTER CHANGED ☐	HARDNESS				
	SANITIZER				
FILTER REPLACED ☐	SHOCK				
	CLARIFIER				
	METAL REDUCER				
5					

NOTES

SPA RECORD

DATE

	FACTOR	INITIAL READING	PRODUCT ADDED	FINAL READING	AMOUNT ADDED
WATER CHARGED ☐	TA				
	PH				
FILTER CHANGED ☐	HARDNESS				
	SANITIZER				
FILTER REPLACED ☐	SHOCK				
	CLARIFIER				
	METAL REDUCER				
5					

NOTES

DATE

	FACTOR	INITIAL READING	PRODUCT ADDED	FINAL READING	AMOUNT ADDED
WATER CHARGED ☐	TA				
	PH				
FILTER CHANGED ☐	HARDNESS				
	SANITIZER				
FILTER REPLACED ☐	SHOCK				
	CLARIFIER				
	METAL REDUCER				
5					

NOTES

POOL / SPA DAILY MAINTENANCE

FACILITY NAME	
FACILITY ADDRESS	
MINIMUM TURNOVER RATE (GPM)	MONTH & YEAR

DATE	CHLORINE RESIDUAL (FREE CHLORINE)	PH	CHEMICALS ADDED (TYPE AND AMOUNT)	TEMP (°F)	OTHER MAINTENANCE (BACKWASH ETC.)
1					
2					
3					
4					
5					
6					
7					
8					
9					
10					
11					
12					
13					
14					
15					
16					
17					
18					
19					
20					
21					
22					
23					
24					
25					
26					
27					
28					
29					
30					
31					

POOL / SPA DAILY MAINTENANCE

FACILITY NAME	
FACILITY ADDRESS	
MINIMUM TURNOVER RATE (GPM)	MONTH & YEAR

DATE	CHLORINE RESIDUAL (FREE CHLORINE)	PH	CHEMICALS ADDED (TYPE AND AMOUNT)	TEMP (°F)	OTHER MAINTENANCE (BACKWASH ETC.)
1					
2					
3					
4					
5					
6					
7					
8					
9					
10					
11					
12					
13					
14					
15					
16					
17					
18					
19					
20					
21					
22					
23					
24					
25					
26					
27					
28					
29					
30					
31					

POOL MAINTENANCE LOG

POOL/CLIENT NAME		DATE	
LOCATION		POOL SIZE	
FLOW RATE REQUIRED		DISINFECTANT TYPE	

DAILY TEST						
	TIME (AM/PM)					
	WATER CLARITY					
	DISINFECTANT PPM					
	COMBINED CHLORINE <50% FREE					
	PH 7.2-8.0					
	FLOW GPM					

WEEKLY TEST						
	ALKALINITY REC RANGE 60-160 PPM					
	CYANURIC ACID IF USED - < 90					

CHEMICALS ADDED						
	QTY OF DISINFECTANT ADDED					
	OTHER CHEMICALS ADDED					

POOL MAINTENANCE LOG

POOL/CLIENT NAME		DATE	
LOCATION		POOL SIZE	
FLOW RATE REQUIRED		DISINFECTANT TYPE	

DAILY TEST							
	TIME (AM/PM)						
	WATER CLARITY						
	DISINFECTANT PPM						
	COMBINED CHLORINE <50% FREE						
	PH 7.2-8.0						
	FLOW GPM						

WEEKLY TEST							
	ALKALINITY REC RANGE 60-160 PPM						
	CYANURIC ACID IF USED - < 90						

CHEMICALS ADDED							
	QTY OF DISINFECTANT ADDED						
	OTHER CHEMICALS ADDED						

POOL MAINTENANCE LOG

MAINTENANCE		
BACKWASH	VACUUM AND/OR BRUSH	CONTAMINANT EPISODE
	☐VACUUM ☐BRUSH	
	☐VACUUM ☐BRUSH	
	☐VACUUM ☐BRUSH	
	☐VACUUM ☐BRUSH	
	☐VACUUM ☐BRUSH	
	☐VACUUM ☐BRUSH	
	☐VACUUM ☐BRUSH	
	☐VACUUM ☐BRUSH	
	☐VACUUM ☐BRUSH	
	☐VACUUM ☐BRUSH	
	☐VACUUM ☐BRUSH	
	☐VACUUM ☐BRUSH	
	☐VACUUM ☐BRUSH	
	☐VACUUM ☐BRUSH	
	☐VACUUM ☐BRUSH	
	☐VACUUM ☐BRUSH	
	☐VACUUM ☐BRUSH	
	☐VACUUM ☐BRUSH	
	☐VACUUM ☐BRUSH	
	☐VACUUM ☐BRUSH	
	☐VACUUM ☐BRUSH	
	☐VACUUM ☐BRUSH	
	☐VACUUM ☐BRUSH	
	☐VACUUM ☐BRUSH	
	☐VACUUM ☐BRUSH	
	☐VACUUM ☐BRUSH	
	☐VACUUM ☐BRUSH	

POOL MAINTENANCE LOG

	MAINTENANCE	
BACKWASH	**VACUUM AND/OR BRUSH**	**CONTAMINANT EPISODE**
	☐VACUUM ☐BRUSH	
	☐VACUUM ☐BRUSH	
	☐VACUUM ☐BRUSH	
	☐VACUUM ☐BRUSH	
	☐VACUUM ☐BRUSH	
	☐VACUUM ☐BRUSH	
	☐VACUUM ☐BRUSH	
	☐VACUUM ☐BRUSH	
	☐VACUUM ☐BRUSH	
	☐VACUUM ☐BRUSH	
	☐VACUUM ☐BRUSH	
	☐VACUUM ☐BRUSH	
	☐VACUUM ☐BRUSH	
	☐VACUUM ☐BRUSH	
	☐VACUUM ☐BRUSH	
	☐VACUUM ☐BRUSH	
	☐VACUUM ☐BRUSH	
	☐VACUUM ☐BRUSH	
	☐VACUUM ☐BRUSH	
	☐VACUUM ☐BRUSH	
	☐VACUUM ☐BRUSH	
	☐VACUUM ☐BRUSH	
	☐VACUUM ☐BRUSH	
	☐VACUUM ☐BRUSH	
	☐VACUUM ☐BRUSH	
	☐VACUUM ☐BRUSH	

MAINTENANCE LOG

DATE		TIME		LAST CHECK	

POOL ID	

CHECKLIST	CHECKED?	VALUE / REMARK
CHECK FILTERS	☐YES ☐NO	
CHECK PUMPS	☐YES ☐NOO	
CHECK WATER TEMPERATURE	☐YES ☐NO	WATER TEMPERATURE:
CHECK WATER LEVEL	☐YES ☐NO	WATER LEVEL:
CHECK WATER FLOW RATE	☐YES ☐NO	WATER FLOW RATE:
WATER PH LEVEL (IDEAL 7.4 - 7.6)	☐YES ☐NO	PH LEVEL:
WATER CHLORINE LEVEL	☐YES ☐NOO	CHLORINE LEVEL:
CHECK OVERALL WATER CLARITY	☐YES ☐NO	
CHECK SKIMMER BASKETS	☐YES ☐NO	
LEAF SKIMMING	☐YES ☐NO	
BRUSH SIDES	☐YES ☐NO	
VACUUM POOL	☐YES ☐NOO	
CHECK CHEMICAL STOCK LEVEL	☐YES ☐NO	ITEMS TO PURCHASE:
CHECK FIRST AID SUPPLIES	☐YES ☐NO	ITEMS NEEDED:
SURROUNDING STRUCTURES CHECK	☐YES ☐NO	CONDITION

CHECKED BY:		SIGNATURE	

MAINTENANCE LOG

DATE		TIME		LAST CHECK	

POOL ID	

CHECKLIST	CHECKED?	VALUE / REMARK
CHECK FILTERS	☐YES ☐NO	
CHECK PUMPS	☐YES ☐NOO	
CHECK WATER TEMPERATURE	☐YES ☐NO	WATER TEMPERATURE:
CHECK WATER LEVEL	☐YES ☐NO	WATER LEVEL:
CHECK WATER FLOW RATE	☐YES ☐NO	WATER FLOW RATE:
WATER PH LEVEL (IDEAL 7.4 - 7.6)	☐YES ☐NO	PH LEVEL:
WATER CHLORINE LEVEL	☐YES ☐NOO	CHLORINE LEVEL:
CHECK OVERALL WATER CLARITY	☐YES ☐NO	
CHECK SKIMMER BASKETS	☐YES ☐NO	
LEAF SKIMMING	☐YES ☐NO	
BRUSH SIDES	☐YES ☐NO	
VACUUM POOL	☐YES ☐NOO	
CHECK CHEMICAL STOCK LEVEL	☐YES ☐NO	ITEMS TO PURCHASE:
CHECK FIRST AID SUPPLIES	☐YES ☐NO	ITEMS NEEDED:
SURROUNDING STRUCTURES CHECK	☐YES ☐NO	CONDITION

CHECKED BY:		SIGNATURE	

SUPPLIES REORDER LIST

DATE		
ITEM		**STOCK NUMBER**

SUPPLIES REORDER LIST

DATE		

ITEM	STOCK NUMBER

SPA INFORMATION RECORD

SPA NAME	
MODEL	

PURCHASE DATE		SERIAL #	
WARRANTY LENGTH		VOLTAGE	☐110 V ☐220 V
GALLONS		OZONATOR	☐YES ☐NO
COVER SIZE		FILTER NUMBER	

FILTER MAINTENANCE RECORD
CLEAN EVERY 3-4 MONTHS, AND WITH EACH WATER CHARGE. REPLACE ANNUALLY.

DATE		CLEANED	REPLACED
		☐	☐
		☐	☐
		☐	☐
		☐	☐
		☐	☐
		☐	☐
		☐	☐

REPAIR RECORD

DATE	DETAILS

SPA INFORMATION RECORD

SPA NAME	
MODEL	

PURCHASE DATE		SERIAL #	
WARRANTY LENGTH		VOLTAGE	☐110 V ☐220 V
GALLONS		OZONATOR	☐YES ☐NO
COVER SIZE		FILTER NUMBER	

FILTER MAINTENANCE RECORD
CLEAN EVERY 3-4 MONTHS, AND WITH EACH WATER CHARGE. REPLACE ANNUALLY.

DATE		CLEANED	REPLACED
		☐	☐
		☐	☐
		☐	☐
		☐	☐
		☐	☐
		☐	☐
		☐	☐

REPAIR RECORD

DATE	DETAILS

SPA RECORD

DATE

	FACTOR	INITIAL READING	PRODUCT ADDED	FINAL READING	AMOUNT ADDED
WATER CHARGED ☐	TA				
	PH				
FILTER CHANGED ☐	HARDNESS				
	SANITIZER				
FILTER REPLACED ☐	SHOCK				
	CLARIFIER				
	METAL REDUCER				
5					

NOTES

DATE

	FACTOR	INITIAL READING	PRODUCT ADDED	FINAL READING	AMOUNT ADDED
WATER CHARGED ☐	TA				
	PH				
FILTER CHANGED ☐	HARDNESS				
	SANITIZER				
FILTER REPLACED ☐	SHOCK				
	CLARIFIER				
	METAL REDUCER				
5					

NOTES

SPA RECORD

DATE

	FACTOR	INITIAL READING	PRODUCT ADDED	FINAL READING	AMOUNT ADDED
WATER CHARGED ☐	TA				
	PH				
FILTER CHANGED ☐	HARDNESS				
	SANITIZER				
FILTER REPLACED ☐	SHOCK				
	CLARIFIER				
	METAL REDUCER				
5					

NOTES

DATE

	FACTOR	INITIAL READING	PRODUCT ADDED	FINAL READING	AMOUNT ADDED
WATER CHARGED ☐	TA				
	PH				
FILTER CHANGED ☐	HARDNESS				
	SANITIZER				
FILTER REPLACED ☐	SHOCK				
	CLARIFIER				
	METAL REDUCER				
5					

NOTES

POOL / SPA DAILY MAINTENANCE

FACILITY NAME	
FACILITY ADDRESS	
MINIMUM TURNOVER RATE (GPM)		MONTH & YEAR	

DATE	CHLORINE RESIDUAL (FREE CHLORINE)	PH	CHEMICALS ADDED (TYPE AND AMOUNT)	TEMP (°F)	OTHER MAINTENANCE (BACKWASH ETC.)
1					
2					
3					
4					
5					
6					
7					
8					
9					
10					
11					
12					
13					
14					
15					
16					
17					
18					
19					
20					
21					
22					
23					
24					
25					
26					
27					
28					
29					
30					
31					

POOL / SPA DAILY MAINTENANCE

FACILITY NAME	
FACILITY ADDRESS	
MINIMUM TURNOVER RATE (GPM)		MONTH & YEAR	

DATE	CHLORINE RESIDUAL (FREE CHLORINE)	PH	CHEMICALS ADDED (TYPE AND AMOUNT)	TEMP (°F)	OTHER MAINTENANCE (BACKWASH ETC.)
1					
2					
3					
4					
5					
6					
7					
8					
9					
10					
11					
12					
13					
14					
15					
16					
17					
18					
19					
20					
21					
22					
23					
24					
25					
26					
27					
28					
29					
30					
31					

POOL MAINTENANCE LOG

POOL/CLIENT NAME		DATE	
LOCATION		POOL SIZE	
FLOW RATE REQUIRED		DISINFECTANT TYPE	

DAILY TEST						
	TIME (AM/PM)					
	WATER CLARITY					
	DISINFECTANT PPM					
	COMBINED CHLORINE <50% FREE					
	PH 7.2-8.0					
	FLOW GPM					

WEEKLY TEST						
	ALKALINITY REC RANGE 60-160 PPM					
	CYANURIC ACID IF USED - < 90					

CHEMICALS ADDED						
	QTY OF DISINFECTANT ADDED					
	OTHER CHEMICALS ADDED					

POOL MAINTENANCE LOG

POOL/CLIENT NAME		DATE	
LOCATION		POOL SIZE	
FLOW RATE REQUIRED		DISINFECTANT TYPE	

DAILY TEST	TIME (AM/PM)					
	WATER CLARITY					
	DISINFECTANT PPM					
	COMBINED CHLORINE <50% FREE					
	PH 7.2-8.0					
	FLOW GPM					

WEEKLY TEST	ALKALINITY REC RANGE 60-160 PPM					
	CYANURIC ACID IF USED - < 90					

CHEMICALS ADDED	QTY OF DISINFECTANT ADDED					
	OTHER CHEMICALS ADDED					

POOL MAINTENANCE LOG

MAINTENANCE		
BACKWASH	**VACUUM AND/OR BRUSH**	**CONTAMINANT EPISODE**
	☐VACUUM ☐BRUSH	
	☐VACUUM ☐BRUSH	
	☐VACUUM ☐BRUSH	
	☐VACUUM ☐BRUSH	
	☐VACUUM ☐BRUSH	
	☐VACUUM ☐BRUSH	
	☐VACUUM ☐BRUSH	
	☐VACUUM ☐BRUSH	
	☐VACUUM ☐BRUSH	
	☐VACUUM ☐BRUSH	
	☐VACUUM ☐BRUSH	
	☐VACUUM ☐BRUSH	
	☐VACUUM ☐BRUSH	
	☐VACUUM ☐BRUSH	
	☐VACUUM ☐BRUSH	
	☐VACUUM ☐BRUSH	
	☐VACUUM ☐BRUSH	
	☐VACUUM ☐BRUSH	
	☐VACUUM ☐BRUSH	
	☐VACUUM ☐BRUSH	
	☐VACUUM ☐BRUSH	
	☐VACUUM ☐BRUSH	
	☐VACUUM ☐BRUSH	
	☐VACUUM ☐BRUSH	
	☐VACUUM ☐BRUSH	
	☐VACUUM ☐BRUSH	
	☐VACUUM ☐BRUSH	

POOL MAINTENANCE LOG

MAINTENANCE		
BACKWASH	**VACUUM AND/OR BRUSH**	**CONTAMINANT EPISODE**
	☐VACUUM ☐BRUSH	
	☐VACUUM ☐BRUSH	
	☐VACUUM ☐BRUSH	
	☐VACUUM ☐BRUSH	
	☐VACUUM ☐BRUSH	
	☐VACUUM ☐BRUSH	
	☐VACUUM ☐BRUSH	
	☐VACUUM ☐BRUSH	
	☐VACUUM ☐BRUSH	
	☐VACUUM ☐BRUSH	
	☐VACUUM ☐BRUSH	
	☐VACUUM ☐BRUSH	
	☐VACUUM ☐BRUSH	
	☐VACUUM ☐BRUSH	
	☐VACUUM ☐BRUSH	
	☐VACUUM ☐BRUSH	
	☐VACUUM ☐BRUSH	
	☐VACUUM ☐BRUSH	
	☐VACUUM ☐BRUSH	
	☐VACUUM ☐BRUSH	
	☐VACUUM ☐BRUSH	
	☐VACUUM ☐BRUSH	
	☐VACUUM ☐BRUSH	
	☐VACUUM ☐BRUSH	
	☐VACUUM ☐BRUSH	
	☐VACUUM ☐BRUSH	

MAINTENANCE LOG

DATE		TIME		LAST CHECK	

POOL ID	

CHECKLIST	CHECKED?	VALUE / REMARK
CHECK FILTERS	☐YES ☐NO	
CHECK PUMPS	☐YES ☐NOO	
CHECK WATER TEMPERATURE	☐YES ☐NO	WATER TEMPERATURE:
CHECK WATER LEVEL	☐YES ☐NO	WATER LEVEL:
CHECK WATER FLOW RATE	☐YES ☐NO	WATER FLOW RATE:
WATER PH LEVEL (IDEAL 7.4 - 7.6)	☐YES ☐NO	PH LEVEL:
WATER CHLORINE LEVEL	☐YES ☐NOO	CHLORINE LEVEL:
CHECK OVERALL WATER CLARITY	☐YES ☐NO	
CHECK SKIMMER BASKETS	☐YES ☐NO	
LEAF SKIMMING	☐YES ☐NO	
BRUSH SIDES	☐YES ☐NO	
VACUUM POOL	☐YES ☐NOO	
CHECK CHEMICAL STOCK LEVEL	☐YES ☐NO	ITEMS TO PURCHASE:
CHECK FIRST AID SUPPLIES	☐YES ☐NO	ITEMS NEEDED:
SURROUNDING STRUCTURES CHECK	☐YES ☐NO	CONDITION

CHECKED BY:		SIGNATURE	

MAINTENANCE LOG

DATE		TIME		LAST CHECK	

POOL ID	

CHECKLIST	CHECKED?	VALUE / REMARK
CHECK FILTERS	☐YES ☐NO	
CHECK PUMPS	☐YES ☐NOO	
CHECK WATER TEMPERATURE	☐YES ☐NO	WATER TEMPERATURE:
CHECK WATER LEVEL	☐YES ☐NO	WATER LEVEL:
CHECK WATER FLOW RATE	☐YES ☐NO	WATER FLOW RATE:
WATER PH LEVEL (IDEAL 7.4 - 7.6)	☐YES ☐NO	PH LEVEL:
WATER CHLORINE LEVEL	☐YES ☐NOO	CHLORINE LEVEL:
CHECK OVERALL WATER CLARITY	☐YES ☐NO	
CHECK SKIMMER BASKETS	☐YES ☐NO	
LEAF SKIMMING	☐YES ☐NO	
BRUSH SIDES	☐YES ☐NO	
VACUUM POOL	☐YES ☐NOO	
CHECK CHEMICAL STOCK LEVEL	☐YES ☐NO	ITEMS TO PURCHASE:
CHECK FIRST AID SUPPLIES	☐YES ☐NO	ITEMS NEEDED:
SURROUNDING STRUCTURES CHECK	☐YES ☐NO	CONDITION

CHECKED BY:		SIGNATURE	

SUPPLIES REORDER LIST

DATE	

ITEM	STOCK NUMBER

SUPPLIES REORDER LIST

DATE		

ITEM	STOCK NUMBER

SPA INFORMATION RECORD

SPA NAME	
MODEL	

PURCHASE DATE		SERIAL #	
WARRANTY LENGTH		VOLTAGE	☐ 110 V ☐ 220 V
GALLONS		OZONATOR	☐ YES ☐ NO
COVER SIZE		FILTER NUMBER	

FILTER MAINTENANCE RECORD
CLEAN EVERY 3-4 MONTHS, AND WITH EACH WATER CHARGE. REPLACE ANNUALLY.

DATE		CLEANED	REPLACED
		☐	☐
		☐	☐
		☐	☐
		☐	☐
		☐	☐
		☐	☐
		☐	☐

REPAIR RECORD

DATE	DETAILS

SPA INFORMATION RECORD

SPA NAME	
MODEL	

PURCHASE DATE		**SERIAL #**	
WARRANTY LENGTH		**VOLTAGE**	☐ 110 V ☐ 220 V
GALLONS		**OZONATOR**	☐ YES ☐ NO
COVER SIZE		**FILTER NUMBER**	

FILTER MAINTENANCE RECORD
CLEAN EVERY 3-4 MONTHS, AND WITH EACH WATER CHARGE. REPLACE ANNUALLY.

DATE		CLEANED	REPLACED
		☐	☐
		☐	☐
		☐	☐
		☐	☐
		☐	☐
		☐	☐
		☐	☐

REPAIR RECORD

DATE	DETAILS

SPA RECORD

DATE

	FACTOR	INITIAL READING	PRODUCT ADDED	FINAL READING	AMOUNT ADDED
WATER CHARGED ☐	TA				
	PH				
FILTER CHANGED ☐	HARDNESS				
	SANITIZER				
FILTER REPLACED ☐	SHOCK				
	CLARIFIER				
	METAL REDUCER				
5					

NOTES

DATE

	FACTOR	INITIAL READING	PRODUCT ADDED	FINAL READING	AMOUNT ADDED
WATER CHARGED ☐	TA				
	PH				
FILTER CHANGED ☐	HARDNESS				
	SANITIZER				
FILTER REPLACED ☐	SHOCK				
	CLARIFIER				
	METAL REDUCER				
5					

NOTES

SPA RECORD

DATE

	FACTOR	INITIAL READING	PRODUCT ADDED	FINAL READING	AMOUNT ADDED
WATER CHARGED ☐	TA				
	PH				
FILTER CHANGED ☐	HARDNESS				
	SANITIZER				
FILTER REPLACED ☐	SHOCK				
	CLARIFIER				
5	METAL REDUCER				

NOTES

DATE

	FACTOR	INITIAL READING	PRODUCT ADDED	FINAL READING	AMOUNT ADDED
WATER CHARGED ☐	TA				
	PH				
FILTER CHANGED ☐	HARDNESS				
	SANITIZER				
FILTER REPLACED ☐	SHOCK				
	CLARIFIER				
5	METAL REDUCER				

NOTES

POOL / SPA DAILY MAINTENANCE

FACILITY NAME	
FACILITY ADDRESS	
MINIMUM TURNOVER RATE (GPM)	MONTH & YEAR

DATE	CHLORINE RESIDUAL (FREE CHLORINE)	PH	CHEMICALS ADDED (TYPE AND AMOUNT)	TEMP (°F)	OTHER MAINTENANCE (BACKWASH ETC.)
1					
2					
3					
4					
5					
6					
7					
8					
9					
10					
11					
12					
13					
14					
15					
16					
17					
18					
19					
20					
21					
22					
23					
24					
25					
26					
27					
28					
29					
30					
31					

POOL / SPA DAILY MAINTENANCE

FACILITY NAME	
FACILITY ADDRESS	
MINIMUM TURNOVER RATE (GPM)	MONTH & YEAR

DATE	CHLORINE RESIDUAL (FREE CHLORINE)	PH	CHEMICALS ADDED (TYPE AND AMOUNT)	TEMP (°F)	OTHER MAINTENANCE (BACKWASH ETC.)
1					
2					
3					
4					
5					
6					
7					
8					
9					
10					
11					
12					
13					
14					
15					
16					
17					
18					
19					
20					
21					
22					
23					
24					
25					
26					
27					
28					
29					
30					
31					

POOL MAINTENANCE LOG

POOL/CLIENT NAME		DATE	
LOCATION		POOL SIZE	
FLOW RATE REQUIRED		DISINFECTANT TYPE	

DAILY TEST						
	TIME (AM/PM)					
	WATER CLARITY					
	DISINFECTANT PPM					
	COMBINED CHLORINE <50% FREE					
	PH 7.2-8.0					
	FLOW GPM					

WEEKLY TEST						
	ALKALINITY REC RANGE 60-160 PPM					
	CYANURIC ACID IF USED - < 90					

CHEMICALS ADDED						
	QTY OF DISINFECTANT ADDED					
	OTHER CHEMICALS ADDED					

POOL MAINTENANCE LOG

POOL/CLIENT NAME		DATE	
LOCATION		POOL SIZE	
FLOW RATE REQUIRED		DISINFECTANT TYPE	

DAILY TEST	TIME (AM/PM)						
	WATER CLARITY						
	DISINFECTANT PPM						
	COMBINED CHLORINE <50% FREE						
	PH 7.2-8.0						
	FLOW GPM						

WEEKLY TEST	ALKALINITY REC RANGE 60-160 PPM						
	CYANURIC ACID IF USED - < 90						

CHEMICALS ADDED	QTY OF DISINFECTANT ADDED						
	OTHER CHEMICALS ADDED						

POOL MAINTENANCE LOG

	MAINTENANCE	
BACKWASH	VACUUM AND/OR BRUSH	CONTAMINANT EPISODE
	☐VACUUM ☐BRUSH	
	☐VACUUM ☐BRUSH	
	☐VACUUM ☐BRUSH	
	☐VACUUM ☐BRUSH	
	☐VACUUM ☐BRUSH	
	☐VACUUM ☐BRUSH	
	☐VACUUM ☐BRUSH	
	☐VACUUM ☐BRUSH	
	☐VACUUM ☐BRUSH	
	☐VACUUM ☐BRUSH	
	☐VACUUM ☐BRUSH	
	☐VACUUM ☐BRUSH	
	☐VACUUM ☐BRUSH	
	☐VACUUM ☐BRUSH	
	☐VACUUM ☐BRUSH	
	☐VACUUM ☐BRUSH	
	☐VACUUM ☐BRUSH	
	☐VACUUM ☐BRUSH	
	☐VACUUM ☐BRUSH	
	☐VACUUM ☐BRUSH	
	☐VACUUM ☐BRUSH	
	☐VACUUM ☐BRUSH	
	☐VACUUM ☐BRUSH	
	☐VACUUM ☐BRUSH	
	☐VACUUM ☐BRUSH	
	☐VACUUM ☐BRUSH	
	☐VACUUM ☐BRUSH	

POOL MAINTENANCE LOG

MAINTENANCE		
BACKWASH	VACUUM AND/OR BRUSH	CONTAMINANT EPISODE
	☐VACUUM ☐BRUSH	
	☐VACUUM ☐BRUSH	
	☐VACUUM ☐BRUSH	
	☐VACUUM ☐BRUSH	
	☐VACUUM ☐BRUSH	
	☐VACUUM ☐BRUSH	
	☐VACUUM ☐BRUSH	
	☐VACUUM ☐BRUSH	
	☐VACUUM ☐BRUSH	
	☐VACUUM ☐BRUSH	
	☐VACUUM ☐BRUSH	
	☐VACUUM ☐BRUSH	
	☐VACUUM ☐BRUSH	
	☐VACUUM ☐BRUSH	
	☐VACUUM ☐BRUSH	
	☐VACUUM ☐BRUSH	
	☐VACUUM ☐BRUSH	
	☐VACUUM ☐BRUSH	
	☐VACUUM ☐BRUSH	
	☐VACUUM ☐BRUSH	
	☐VACUUM ☐BRUSH	
	☐VACUUM ☐BRUSH	
	☐VACUUM ☐BRUSH	
	☐VACUUM ☐BRUSH	
	☐VACUUM ☐BRUSH	
	☐VACUUM ☐BRUSH	

MAINTENANCE LOG

DATE		TIME		LAST CHECK	

POOL ID	

CHECKLIST	CHECKED?	VALUE / REMARK
CHECK FILTERS	☐YES ☐NO	
CHECK PUMPS	☐YES ☐NOO	
CHECK WATER TEMPERATURE	☐YES ☐NO	WATER TEMPERATURE:
CHECK WATER LEVEL	☐YES ☐NO	WATER LEVEL:
CHECK WATER FLOW RATE	☐YES ☐NO	WATER FLOW RATE:
WATER PH LEVEL (IDEAL 7.4 - 7.6)	☐YES ☐NO	PH LEVEL:
WATER CHLORINE LEVEL	☐YES ☐NOO	CHLORINE LEVEL:
CHECK OVERALL WATER CLARITY	☐YES ☐NO	
CHECK SKIMMER BASKETS	☐YES ☐NO	
LEAF SKIMMING	☐YES ☐NO	
BRUSH SIDES	☐YES ☐NO	
VACUUM POOL	☐YES ☐NOO	
CHECK CHEMICAL STOCK LEVEL	☐YES ☐NO	ITEMS TO PURCHASE:
CHECK FIRST AID SUPPLIES	☐YES ☐NO	ITEMS NEEDED:
SURROUNDING STRUCTURES CHECK	☐YES ☐NO	CONDITION

CHECKED BY:		SIGNATURE	

MAINTENANCE LOG

DATE		TIME		LAST CHECK	

POOL ID	

CHECKLIST	CHECKED?	VALUE / REMARK
CHECK FILTERS	☐YES ☐NO	
CHECK PUMPS	☐YES ☐NOO	
CHECK WATER TEMPERATURE	☐YES ☐NO	WATER TEMPERATURE:
CHECK WATER LEVEL	☐YES ☐NO	WATER LEVEL:
CHECK WATER FLOW RATE	☐YES ☐NO	WATER FLOW RATE:
WATER PH LEVEL (IDEAL 7.4 - 7.6)	☐YES ☐NO	PH LEVEL:
WATER CHLORINE LEVEL	☐YES ☐NOO	CHLORINE LEVEL:
CHECK OVERALL WATER CLARITY	☐YES ☐NO	
CHECK SKIMMER BASKETS	☐YES ☐NO	
LEAF SKIMMING	☐YES ☐NO	
BRUSH SIDES	☐YES ☐NO	
VACUUM POOL	☐YES ☐NOO	
CHECK CHEMICAL STOCK LEVEL	☐YES ☐NO	ITEMS TO PURCHASE:
CHECK FIRST AID SUPPLIES	☐YES ☐NO	ITEMS NEEDED:
SURROUNDING STRUCTURES CHECK	☐YES ☐NO	CONDITION

CHECKED BY:		SIGNATURE	

SUPPLIES REORDER LIST

DATE		
ITEM		**STOCK NUMBER**

SUPPLIES REORDER LIST

DATE		

ITEM	STOCK NUMBER

SPA INFORMATION RECORD

SPA NAME	
MODEL	

PURCHASE DATE		**SERIAL #**	
WARRANTY LENGTH		**VOLTAGE**	☐ 110 V ☐ 220 V
GALLONS		**OZONATOR**	☐ YES ☐ NO
COVER SIZE		**FILTER NUMBER**	

FILTER MAINTENANCE RECORD
CLEAN EVERY 3-4 MONTHS, AND WITH EACH WATER CHARGE. REPLACE ANNUALLY.

DATE		CLEANED	REPLACED
		☐	☐
		☐	☐
		☐	☐
		☐	☐
		☐	☐
		☐	☐
		☐	☐

REPAIR RECORD

DATE	DETAILS

SPA INFORMATION RECORD

SPA NAME			
MODEL			
PURCHASE DATE		SERIAL #	
WARRANTY LENGTH		VOLTAGE	☐ 110 V ☐ 220 V
GALLONS		OZONATOR	☐ YES ☐ NO
COVER SIZE		FILTER NUMBER	

FILTER MAINTENANCE RECORD
CLEAN EVERY 3-4 MONTHS, AND WITH EACH WATER CHARGE. REPLACE ANNUALLY.

DATE		CLEANED	REPLACED
		☐	☐
		☐	☐
		☐	☐
		☐	☐
		☐	☐
		☐	☐
		☐	☐

REPAIR RECORD

DATE	DETAILS

SPA RECORD

DATE

	FACTOR	INITIAL READING	PRODUCT ADDED	FINAL READING	AMOUNT ADDED
WATER CHARGED ☐	TA				
	PH				
FILTER CHANGED ☐	HARDNESS				
	SANITIZER				
FILTER REPLACED ☐	SHOCK				
	CLARIFIER				
5	METAL REDUCER				

NOTES

DATE

	FACTOR	INITIAL READING	PRODUCT ADDED	FINAL READING	AMOUNT ADDED
WATER CHARGED ☐	TA				
	PH				
FILTER CHANGED ☐	HARDNESS				
	SANITIZER				
FILTER REPLACED ☐	SHOCK				
	CLARIFIER				
5	METAL REDUCER				

NOTES

SPA RECORD

DATE

	FACTOR	INITIAL READING	PRODUCT ADDED	FINAL READING	AMOUNT ADDED
WATER CHARGED ☐	TA				
	PH				
FILTER CHANGED ☐	HARDNESS				
	SANITIZER				
FILTER REPLACED ☐	SHOCK				
	CLARIFIER				
5	METAL REDUCER				

NOTES

DATE

	FACTOR	INITIAL READING	PRODUCT ADDED	FINAL READING	AMOUNT ADDED
WATER CHARGED ☐	TA				
	PH				
FILTER CHANGED ☐	HARDNESS				
	SANITIZER				
FILTER REPLACED ☐	SHOCK				
	CLARIFIER				
5	METAL REDUCER				

NOTES

POOL / SPA DAILY MAINTENANCE

FACILITY NAME					
FACILITY ADDRESS					
MINIMUM TURNOVER RATE (GPM)				MONTH & YEAR	

DATE	CHLORINE RESIDUAL (FREE CHLORINE)	PH	CHEMICALS ADDED (TYPE AND AMOUNT)	TEMP (°F)	OTHER MAINTENANCE (BACKWASH ETC.)
1					
2					
3					
4					
5					
6					
7					
8					
9					
10					
11					
12					
13					
14					
15					
16					
17					
18					
19					
20					
21					
22					
23					
24					
25					
26					
27					
28					
29					
30					
31					

POOL / SPA DAILY MAINTENANCE

FACILITY NAME					
FACILITY ADDRESS					
MINIMUM TURNOVER RATE (GPM)			MONTH & YEAR		

DATE	CHLORINE RESIDUAL (FREE CHLORINE)	PH	CHEMICALS ADDED (TYPE AND AMOUNT)	TEMP (°F)	OTHER MAINTENANCE (BACKWASH ETC.)
1					
2					
3					
4					
5					
6					
7					
8					
9					
10					
11					
12					
13					
14					
15					
16					
17					
18					
19					
20					
21					
22					
23					
24					
25					
26					
27					
28					
29					
30					
31					

POOL MAINTENANCE LOG

POOL/CLIENT NAME		DATE	
LOCATION		POOL SIZE	
FLOW RATE REQUIRED		DISINFECTANT TYPE	

DAILY TEST	TIME (AM/PM)					
	WATER CLARITY					
	DISINFECTANT PPM					
	COMBINED CHLORINE <50% FREE					
	PH 7.2-8.0					
	FLOW GPM					

WEEKLY TEST	ALKALINITY REC RANGE 60-160 PPM					
	CYANURIC ACID IF USED - < 90					

CHEMICALS ADDED	QTY OF DISINFECTANT ADDED					
	OTHER CHEMICALS ADDED					

POOL MAINTENANCE LOG

POOL/CLIENT NAME		DATE	
LOCATION		POOL SIZE	
FLOW RATE REQUIRED		DISINFECTANT TYPE	

DAILY TEST							
	TIME (AM/PM)						
	WATER CLARITY						
	DISINFECTANT PPM						
	COMBINED CHLORINE <50% FREE						
	PH 7.2-8.0						
	FLOW GPM						

WEEKLY TEST							
	ALKALINITY REC RANGE 60-160 PPM						
	CYANURIC ACID IF USED - < 90						

CHEMICALS ADDED							
	QTY OF DISINFECTANT ADDED						
	OTHER CHEMICALS ADDED						

POOL MAINTENANCE LOG

	MAINTENANCE	
BACKWASH	**VACUUM AND/OR BRUSH**	**CONTAMINANT EPISODE**
	☐ VACUUM ☐ BRUSH	
	☐ VACUUM ☐ BRUSH	
	☐ VACUUM ☐ BRUSH	
	☐ VACUUM ☐ BRUSH	
	☐ VACUUM ☐ BRUSH	
	☐ VACUUM ☐ BRUSH	
	☐ VACUUM ☐ BRUSH	
	☐ VACUUM ☐ BRUSH	
	☐ VACUUM ☐ BRUSH	
	☐ VACUUM ☐ BRUSH	
	☐ VACUUM ☐ BRUSH	
	☐ VACUUM ☐ BRUSH	
	☐ VACUUM ☐ BRUSH	
	☐ VACUUM ☐ BRUSH	
	☐ VACUUM ☐ BRUSH	
	☐ VACUUM ☐ BRUSH	
	☐ VACUUM ☐ BRUSH	
	☐ VACUUM ☐ BRUSH	
	☐ VACUUM ☐ BRUSH	
	☐ VACUUM ☐ BRUSH	
	☐ VACUUM ☐ BRUSH	
	☐ VACUUM ☐ BRUSH	
	☐ VACUUM ☐ BRUSH	
	☐ VACUUM ☐ BRUSH	
	☐ VACUUM ☐ BRUSH	
	☐ VACUUM ☐ BRUSH	

POOL MAINTENANCE LOG

MAINTENANCE		
BACKWASH	VACUUM AND/OR BRUSH	CONTAMINANT EPISODE
	☐VACUUM ☐BRUSH	
	☐VACUUM ☐BRUSH	
	☐VACUUM ☐BRUSH	
	☐VACUUM ☐BRUSH	
	☐VACUUM ☐BRUSH	
	☐VACUUM ☐BRUSH	
	☐VACUUM ☐BRUSH	
	☐VACUUM ☐BRUSH	
	☐VACUUM ☐BRUSH	
	☐VACUUM ☐BRUSH	
	☐VACUUM ☐BRUSH	
	☐VACUUM ☐BRUSH	
	☐VACUUM ☐BRUSH	
	☐VACUUM ☐BRUSH	
	☐VACUUM ☐BRUSH	
	☐VACUUM ☐BRUSH	
	☐VACUUM ☐BRUSH	
	☐VACUUM ☐BRUSH	
	☐VACUUM ☐BRUSH	
	☐VACUUM ☐BRUSH	
	☐VACUUM ☐BRUSH	
	☐VACUUM ☐BRUSH	
	☐VACUUM ☐BRUSH	
	☐VACUUM ☐BRUSH	
	☐VACUUM ☐BRUSH	
	☐VACUUM ☐BRUSH	
	☐VACUUM ☐BRUSH	

MAINTENANCE LOG

DATE		TIME		LAST CHECK	

POOL ID	

CHECKLIST	CHECKED?	VALUE / REMARK
CHECK FILTERS	☐YES ☐NO	
CHECK PUMPS	☐YES ☐NOO	
CHECK WATER TEMPERATURE	☐YES ☐NO	WATER TEMPERATURE:
CHECK WATER LEVEL	☐YES ☐NO	WATER LEVEL:
CHECK WATER FLOW RATE	☐YES ☐NO	WATER FLOW RATE:
WATER PH LEVEL (IDEAL 7.4 - 7.6)	☐YES ☐NO	PH LEVEL:
WATER CHLORINE LEVEL	☐YES ☐NOO	CHLORINE LEVEL:
CHECK OVERALL WATER CLARITY	☐YES ☐NO	
CHECK SKIMMER BASKETS	☐YES ☐NO	
LEAF SKIMMING	☐YES ☐NO	
BRUSH SIDES	☐YES ☐NO	
VACUUM POOL	☐YES ☐NOO	
CHECK CHEMICAL STOCK LEVEL	☐YES ☐NO	ITEMS TO PURCHASE:
CHECK FIRST AID SUPPLIES	☐YES ☐NO	ITEMS NEEDED:
SURROUNDING STRUCTURES CHECK	☐YES ☐NO	CONDITION

CHECKED BY:		SIGNATURE	

MAINTENANCE LOG

DATE		TIME		LAST CHECK	

POOL ID	

CHECKLIST	CHECKED?	VALUE / REMARK
CHECK FILTERS	☐YES ☐NO	
CHECK PUMPS	☐YES ☐NOO	
CHECK WATER TEMPERATURE	☐YES ☐NO	WATER TEMPERATURE:
CHECK WATER LEVEL	☐YES ☐NO	WATER LEVEL:
CHECK WATER FLOW RATE	☐YES ☐NO	WATER FLOW RATE:
WATER PH LEVEL (IDEAL 7.4 - 7.6)	☐YES ☐NO	PH LEVEL:
WATER CHLORINE LEVEL	☐YES ☐NOO	CHLORINE LEVEL:
CHECK OVERALL WATER CLARITY	☐YES ☐NO	
CHECK SKIMMER BASKETS	☐YES ☐NO	
LEAF SKIMMING	☐YES ☐NO	
BRUSH SIDES	☐YES ☐NO	
VACUUM POOL	☐YES ☐NOO	
CHECK CHEMICAL STOCK LEVEL	☐YES ☐NO	ITEMS TO PURCHASE:
CHECK FIRST AID SUPPLIES	☐YES ☐NO	ITEMS NEEDED:
SURROUNDING STRUCTURES CHECK	☐YES ☐NO	CONDITION

CHECKED BY:		SIGNATURE	

SUPPLIES REORDER LIST

DATE		

ITEM	STOCK NUMBER

SUPPLIES REORDER LIST

DATE		
ITEM		**STOCK NUMBER**

SPA INFORMATION RECORD

SPA NAME	
MODEL	

PURCHASE DATE		SERIAL #	
WARRANTY LENGTH		VOLTAGE	☐110 V ☐220 V
GALLONS		OZONATOR	☐YES ☐NO
COVER SIZE		FILTER NUMBER	

FILTER MAINTENANCE RECORD
CLEAN EVERY 3-4 MONTHS, AND WITH EACH WATER CHARGE. REPLACE ANNUALLY.

DATE		CLEANED	REPLACED
		☐	☐
		☐	☐
		☐	☐
		☐	☐
		☐	☐
		☐	☐
		☐	☐

REPAIR RECORD

DATE	DETAILS

SPA INFORMATION RECORD

SPA NAME			
MODEL			
PURCHASE DATE		**SERIAL #**	
WARRANTY LENGTH		**VOLTAGE**	☐110 V ☐220 V
GALLONS		**OZONATOR**	☐YES ☐NO
COVER SIZE		**FILTER NUMBER**	

FILTER MAINTENANCE RECORD
CLEAN EVERY 3-4 MONTHS, AND WITH EACH WATER CHARGE. REPLACE ANNUALLY.

DATE		CLEANED	REPLACED
		☐	☐
		☐	☐
		☐	☐
		☐	☐
		☐	☐
		☐	☐
		☐	☐

REPAIR RECORD

DATE	DETAILS

SPA RECORD

DATE

	FACTOR	INITIAL READING	PRODUCT ADDED	FINAL READING	AMOUNT ADDED
WATER CHARGED ☐	TA				
	PH				
FILTER CHANGED ☐	HARDNESS				
	SANITIZER				
FILTER REPLACED ☐	SHOCK				
	CLARIFIER				
5	METAL REDUCER				

NOTES

DATE

	FACTOR	INITIAL READING	PRODUCT ADDED	FINAL READING	AMOUNT ADDED
WATER CHARGED ☐	TA				
	PH				
FILTER CHANGED ☐	HARDNESS				
	SANITIZER				
FILTER REPLACED ☐	SHOCK				
	CLARIFIER				
5	METAL REDUCER				

NOTES

SPA RECORD

DATE

	FACTOR	INITIAL READING	PRODUCT ADDED	FINAL READING	AMOUNT ADDED
WATER CHARGED ☐	TA				
	PH				
FILTER CHANGED ☐	HARDNESS				
	SANITIZER				
FILTER REPLACED ☐	SHOCK				
	CLARIFIER				
5	METAL REDUCER				

NOTES

DATE

	FACTOR	INITIAL READING	PRODUCT ADDED	FINAL READING	AMOUNT ADDED
WATER CHARGED ☐	TA				
	PH				
FILTER CHANGED ☐	HARDNESS				
	SANITIZER				
FILTER REPLACED ☐	SHOCK				
	CLARIFIER				
5	METAL REDUCER				

NOTES

POOL / SPA DAILY MAINTENANCE

FACILITY NAME	
FACILITY ADDRESS	
MINIMUM TURNOVER RATE (GPM)	MONTH & YEAR

DATE	CHLORINE RESIDUAL (FREE CHLORINE)	PH	CHEMICALS ADDED (TYPE AND AMOUNT)	TEMP (°F)	OTHER MAINTENANCE (BACKWASH ETC.)
1					
2					
3					
4					
5					
6					
7					
8					
9					
10					
11					
12					
13					
14					
15					
16					
17					
18					
19					
20					
21					
22					
23					
24					
25					
26					
27					
28					
29					
30					
31					

POOL / SPA DAILY MAINTENANCE

FACILITY NAME	
FACILITY ADDRESS	
MINIMUM TURNOVER RATE (GPM)	MONTH & YEAR

DATE	CHLORINE RESIDUAL (FREE CHLORINE)	PH	CHEMICALS ADDED (TYPE AND AMOUNT)	TEMP (°F)	OTHER MAINTENANCE (BACKWASH ETC.)
1					
2					
3					
4					
5					
6					
7					
8					
9					
10					
11					
12					
13					
14					
15					
16					
17					
18					
19					
20					
21					
22					
23					
24					
25					
26					
27					
28					
29					
30					
31					

POOL MAINTENANCE LOG

POOL/CLIENT NAME		DATE	
LOCATION		POOL SIZE	
FLOW RATE REQUIRED		DISINFECTANT TYPE	

DAILY TEST	TIME (AM/PM)					
	WATER CLARITY					
	DISINFECTANT PPM					
	COMBINED CHLORINE <50% FREE					
	PH 7.2-8.0					
	FLOW GPM					

WEEKLY TEST	ALKALINITY REC RANGE 60-160 PPM					
	CYANURIC ACID IF USED - < 90					

CHEMICALS ADDED	QTY OF DISINFECTANT ADDED					
	OTHER CHEMICALS ADDED					

POOL MAINTENANCE LOG

POOL/CLIENT NAME		DATE	
LOCATION		POOL SIZE	
FLOW RATE REQUIRED		DISINFECTANT TYPE	

DAILY TEST	TIME (AM/PM)						
	WATER CLARITY						
	DISINFECTANT PPM						
	COMBINED CHLORINE <50% FREE						
	PH 7.2-8.0						
	FLOW GPM						

WEEKLY TEST	ALKALINITY REC RANGE 60-160 PPM						
	CYANURIC ACID IF USED - < 90						

CHEMICALS ADDED	QTY OF DISINFECTANT ADDED						
	OTHER CHEMICALS ADDED						

POOL MAINTENANCE LOG

	MAINTENANCE	
BACKWASH	VACUUM AND/OR BRUSH	CONTAMINANT EPISODE
	☐VACUUM ☐BRUSH	
	☐VACUUM ☐BRUSH	
	☐VACUUM ☐BRUSH	
	☐VACUUM ☐BRUSH	
	☐VACUUM ☐BRUSH	
	☐VACUUM ☐BRUSH	
	☐VACUUM ☐BRUSH	
	☐VACUUM ☐BRUSH	
	☐VACUUM ☐BRUSH	
	☐VACUUM ☐BRUSH	
	☐VACUUM ☐BRUSH	
	☐VACUUM ☐BRUSH	
	☐VACUUM ☐BRUSH	
	☐VACUUM ☐BRUSH	
	☐VACUUM ☐BRUSH	
	☐VACUUM ☐BRUSH	
	☐VACUUM ☐BRUSH	
	☐VACUUM ☐BRUSH	
	☐VACUUM ☐BRUSH	
	☐VACUUM ☐BRUSH	
	☐VACUUM ☐BRUSH	
	☐VACUUM ☐BRUSH	
	☐VACUUM ☐BRUSH	
	☐VACUUM ☐BRUSH	
	☐VACUUM ☐BRUSH	
	☐VACUUM ☐BRUSH	

POOL MAINTENANCE LOG

	MAINTENANCE	
BACKWASH	VACUUM AND/OR BRUSH	CONTAMINANT EPISODE
	☐VACUUM ☐BRUSH	
	☐VACUUM ☐BRUSH	
	☐VACUUM ☐BRUSH	
	☐VACUUM ☐BRUSH	
	☐VACUUM ☐BRUSH	
	☐VACUUM ☐BRUSH	
	☐VACUUM ☐BRUSH	
	☐VACUUM ☐BRUSH	
	☐VACUUM ☐BRUSH	
	☐VACUUM ☐BRUSH	
	☐VACUUM ☐BRUSH	
	☐VACUUM ☐BRUSH	
	☐VACUUM ☐BRUSH	
	☐VACUUM ☐BRUSH	
	☐VACUUM ☐BRUSH	
	☐VACUUM ☐BRUSH	
	☐VACUUM ☐BRUSH	
	☐VACUUM ☐BRUSH	
	☐VACUUM ☐BRUSH	
	☐VACUUM ☐BRUSH	
	☐VACUUM ☐BRUSH	
	☐VACUUM ☐BRUSH	
	☐VACUUM ☐BRUSH	
	☐VACUUM ☐BRUSH	
	☐VACUUM ☐BRUSH	
	☐VACUUM ☐BRUSH	
	☐VACUUM ☐BRUSH	

MAINTENANCE LOG

DATE		TIME		LAST CHECK	
POOL ID					

CHECKLIST	CHECKED?	VALUE / REMARK
CHECK FILTERS	☐YES ☐NO	
CHECK PUMPS	☐YES ☐NOO	
CHECK WATER TEMPERATURE	☐YES ☐NO	WATER TEMPERATURE:
CHECK WATER LEVEL	☐YES ☐NO	WATER LEVEL:
CHECK WATER FLOW RATE	☐YES ☐NO	WATER FLOW RATE:
WATER PH LEVEL (IDEAL 7.4 - 7.6)	☐YES ☐NO	PH LEVEL:
WATER CHLORINE LEVEL	☐YES ☐NOO	CHLORINE LEVEL:
CHECK OVERALL WATER CLARITY	☐YES ☐NO	
CHECK SKIMMER BASKETS	☐YES ☐NO	
LEAF SKIMMING	☐YES ☐NO	
BRUSH SIDES	☐YES ☐NO	
VACUUM POOL	☐YES ☐NOO	
CHECK CHEMICAL STOCK LEVEL	☐YES ☐NO	ITEMS TO PURCHASE:
CHECK FIRST AID SUPPLIES	☐YES ☐NO	ITEMS NEEDED:
SURROUNDING STRUCTURES CHECK	☐YES ☐NO	CONDITION

CHECKED BY:		SIGNATURE	

MAINTENANCE LOG

DATE		TIME		LAST CHECK	

POOL ID	

CHECKLIST	CHECKED?	VALUE / REMARK
CHECK FILTERS	☐YES ☐NO	
CHECK PUMPS	☐YES ☐NOO	
CHECK WATER TEMPERATURE	☐YES ☐NO	WATER TEMPERATURE:
CHECK WATER LEVEL	☐YES ☐NO	WATER LEVEL:
CHECK WATER FLOW RATE	☐YES ☐NO	WATER FLOW RATE:
WATER PH LEVEL (IDEAL 7.4 - 7.6)	☐YES ☐NO	PH LEVEL:
WATER CHLORINE LEVEL	☐YES ☐NOO	CHLORINE LEVEL:
CHECK OVERALL WATER CLARITY	☐YES ☐NO	
CHECK SKIMMER BASKETS	☐YES ☐NO	
LEAF SKIMMING	☐YES ☐NO	
BRUSH SIDES	☐YES ☐NO	
VACUUM POOL	☐YES ☐NOO	
CHECK CHEMICAL STOCK LEVEL	☐YES ☐NO	ITEMS TO PURCHASE:
CHECK FIRST AID SUPPLIES	☐YES ☐NO	ITEMS NEEDED:
SURROUNDING STRUCTURES CHECK	☐YES ☐NO	CONDITION

CHECKED BY:		SIGNATURE	

SUPPLIES REORDER LIST

DATE		
ITEM		**STOCK NUMBER**

SUPPLIES REORDER LIST

DATE		
ITEM		**STOCK NUMBER**